# Instant OSGi Starter

The essential guide to modular development with OSGi

Johan Edstrom

Jamie Goodyear

PUBLISHING

BIRMINGHAM - MUMBAI

# Instant OSGi Starter

First published: January 2013

Production Reference: 1170113

Published by Packt Publishing Ltd.
Livery Place
35 Livery Street
Birmingham B3 2PB, UK.

ISBN 978-1-84951-992-2

www.packtpub.com

# Credits

**Authors**

Johan Edstrom

Jamie Goodyear

**Reviewer**

Tomek Lipski

**Acquisition Editor**

Joanna Finchen

**Commissioning Editor**

Meeta Rajani

**Technical Editors**

Ameya Sawant

Vrinda Amberkar

**Copy Editor**

Alfida Paiva

**Project Coordinator**

Michelle Quadros

**Proofreader**

Maria Gould

**Graphics**

Aditi Gajjar

**Production Coordinator**

Prachali Bhiwandkar

**Cover Work**

Prachali Bhiwandkar

**Cover Image**

Conidon Miranda

# About the authors

**Johan Edstrom** is an open source software evangelist, Apache developer, and a seasoned architect working with Savoir Technologies. He has created Java architectures for large and scalable, high transaction monitoring, financial, and open source systems. He has worked as a development lead, an infrastructure manager, an IT lead, and a programmer. He has also guided several large companies to succeed in the use of open source software components. Lately, he has been helping some of the world's largest networking companies and medical startups in achieving high availability, scalability, and dynamically adapting SOA systems. Johan divides his time between writing software, mentoring development teams, and teaching people how to use Apache ServiceMix, Camel, CXF, and ActiveMQ effectively and make them scalable for enterprise installations.

Johan blogs at `http://johan-edstrom.blogspot.com/`.

**Jamie Goodyear** is an Apache developer and computer systems analyst working with Savoir Technologies. He has designed and critiqued architectures for large organizations worldwide. He has worked as a systems administrator, a software quality assurance tester, and a senior software developer. He has attained the committer status on Apache Karaf, ServiceMix, and Felix, and is a Project Management Committee member for Apache Karaf. Jamie divides his time between providing high-level reviews of architectures, helping to grow the Apache Karaf community, and teaching developers about the Apache Way.

Jamie blogs at `http://icodebythesea.blogspot.com/`.

# About the reviewer

**Tomek Lipski** is a Polyglot programmer, and an open source enthusiast and evangelist. He has over 16 years of commercial experience in IT and 10 years of working experience in integration, VAS, and traditional IT areas for the biggest companies in Central Europe.

In 2011, he designed and coordinated an implementation and launch of Aperte Workflow—an open source BPMS. Aperte Workflow utilizes the OSGi plugin management system to provide flexible solutions, combining several popular open source Java-based technologies such as Liferay, Vaadin, and Activiti.

# www.packtpub.com

## Support files, eBooks, discount offers and more

You might want to visit www.PacktPub.com for support files and downloads related to your book.

Did you know that Packt offers eBook versions of every book published, with PDF and ePub files available? You can upgrade to the eBook version at www.PacktPub.com and as a print book customer, you are entitled to a discount on the eBook copy. Get in touch with us at service@packtpub.com for more details.

At www.PacktPub.com, you can also read a collection of free technical articles, sign up for a range of free newsletters and receive exclusive discounts and offers on Packt books and eBooks.

# packtLib.packtpub.com

Do you need instant solutions to your IT questions? PacktLib is Packt's online digital book library. Here, you can access, read and search across Packt's entire library of books.

## Why Subscribe?

+ Fully searchable across every book published by Packt
+ Copy and paste, print and bookmark content
+ On demand and accessible via web browser

## Free Access for Packt account holders

If you have an account with Packt at www.PacktPub.com, you can use this to access PacktLib today and view nine entirely free books. Simply use your login credentials for immediate access.

# Table of Contents

# Instant OSGi Starter

Welcome to the *Instant OSGi Starter*. This book has been created especially to provide you with all the information that you need to set up OSGi. You will learn the basics, get started with building your first OSGi application, and discover some tips and tricks for using OSGi.

This book contains the following sections:

*So, what is OSGi?* – Find out what you can do with it, and what it can bring to your development infrastructure. OSGi is generally seen as being very complex, with many moving parts; our goal is to reduce this.

*Installation* – OSGi brings many runtime benefits, but before we get there we'll use several tools and technologies to build modular Java applications. BND tool, Apache Maven, Apache Karaf, Eclipse Virgo, Blueprint, and Pax Exam will be discussed.

*Quick start – your first OSGi bundles* – This section will get you started on programming with OSGi. We'll provide you with an example that includes creating a bundle with activator, connecting to the service registry, and constructing service consumers. We'll also provide a brief sample of using Pax Exam to test the sample system.

*Top five features you'll want to know about* – OSGi's three-layered design promotes modularity. However, your application needs to be architected towards modularity, simplicity, and there-use of common resources. In this section, we'll learn some of the basic tenets of modular code practices.

*People and places you should get to know* – There are many communities on the Internet that are working towards bettering modular programming and OSGi; it is here that you can find resources as well as help for your possible OSGi woes. This section provides you with many useful links to the project communities as well as the ongoing work.

# So, what is OSGi?

In this section you'll find out what OSGi actually is, what you can do with it, and what it can bring to your development infrastructure. OSGi is a modular runtime for applications requiring a life cycle, deployment into a running container as well as re-use of services and libraries. OSGi is often seen as being complex, with many tooling and classloading issues. Our goal is to show you how to overcome these issues which are often misconceived. If you take the time up front, building applications is actually quite simple.

The basic function of OSGi is to provide Java developers with a component model that regulates code identity, versioning, interaction between code, life cycle, and making code requirements strictly enforceable. This model is encapsulated by its three key aspects; bundles, life cycle, and services—all within a single OSGi container. See the OSGi home page `http://www.osgi.org/Specifications/HomePage` for the full specification. OSGi is a very mature standard; the original OSGi Service Gateway Specification Release 1.0 was released in May 2000. The key architectural aspects of OSGi that we will be focusing on is shown in the following diagram:

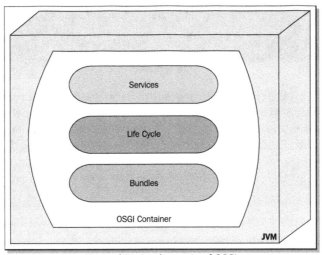

Key architectural aspects of OSGi

## What kind of things can you do with OSGi?

OSGi allows you to create dynamic, live architectures and applications.

Starting with bundles, developers are able to encapsulate functional portions of code into single deployable units, with explicitly stated imported and exported packages. This allows for simplified management since the bundle has a clear function and environment. A **bundle** is a jar with additional information. This information allows you to control what packages are imported, exported, as well as which ones are private and/or hidden. In contrast to a regular classloading environment, you as a developer can control explicitly what you expose, share, and how it is versioned.

It also motivates you as a developer to build distinctly identifiable JAR files, small sets of code that do a few things in a clearly defined manner.

OSGi provides these bundles with a life cycle. Despite OSGi's age, it is still one of the few plugin solutions that actually implement this correctly, allowing you to load and unload as you need. Once a bundle is resolved it can be freely started or stopped, updated, or removed remotely via an API. The framework handles the heavy lifting, ensuring that an installed bundle has all of its requirements met. The following screenshot shows Apache Karaf which wraps an OSGi core, providing developers with a simple interface to manage their OSGi applications:

Apache Karaf

Finally, OSGi allows developers to take advantage of micro-services; these are services provided by one bundle to another in a dynamic fashion. As bundles come and go in the framework, the wiring between service producers and consumers is managed such that bundles adapt to the changing environment. This is a very empowering feature indeed, allowing developers to build nearly organic architectures that evolve after initial deployment at runtime, not to mention a holy grail of factory patterns for applications that need to grow.

## How can you use OSGi within your existing applications?

OSGi is best used with applications designed using modular programming principles; however, your existing Java-based applications can take advantage of OSGi. When we look closer at OSGi applications we'll see that very little or no additional code is required to make aspects of OSGi available to your application. The essential addition is a few extra headers added to Java Archive manifest files. These headers are used to identify the bundle, its version, its imported dependencies from the environment, and any exported packages the bundle provides. In fact, just adding these few OSGi headers to a JAR manifest will create a valid OSGi bundle. To take advantage of more advanced OSGi features, however, we'll have to introduce some additional code; luckily the additions will not introduce a heavy burden on developers. Let's continue onwards and explore how to set up an OSGi environment, then we'll dive into building a complete OSGi application.

# Installation

In three easy steps, you can install an OSGI framework and get it set up on your system. A bare OSGi core however can be unwieldy; therefore we'll show you how to install Apache Karaf as an OSGi environment (steps 4 and 5), as well as how to obtain the BND tool to help make OSGi bundles (step 6), a blueprint for handing services (step 7), and finally Pax Exam for testing your applications (step 8). We've chosen to include Apache Karaf instructions, as we believe it to be an easier environment to be introduced to OSGi, and interact with a running core. You should note that you may also find success using BND, Apache Ant, BNDTools, and Eclipse IDE; coverage of all possible OSGi development tool chains is beyond the scope of this book.

## Step 1 – what do I need?

Before you install OSGi, you will need to check that you have all of the required elements, listed as follows:

+ Disk space: 20 MB free (minimum). You will require more free space as additional resources are provisioned into the OSGi container.

+ Memory: 128 MB (minimum), 2GB+ (recommended).

+ OSGi frameworks are written in Java. Currently, OSGi rev 4.2 implementations from Apache Felix require a minimum of Java 1.4 to run.

+ We'll make use of Apache Maven 2.2.1 for provisioning and building automation.

+ For our demos we'll use Apache Karaf 2.2.8 as an OSGi runtime environment. This will simplify getting introduced to OSGi, as an interactive shell is provided, and users can easily switch OSGi cores.

## Step 2 – downloading an OSGi core

The easiest way to download an OSGi core is as a compressed package from `http://felix.apache.org/site/downloads.cgi`.

We suggest that you download the most current stable build. For our purposes we'll focus on Apache Felix. After downloading and unpacking the archive, you will be left with a directory called `felix-framework-4.0.2`, containing a number of files and folders. Among these there will be a `bin` folder, which contains the Felix OSGi core JAR file (`org.apache.felix.main.distribution-4.0.2.tar.gz`). The following screenshot shows the Apache Felix download page:

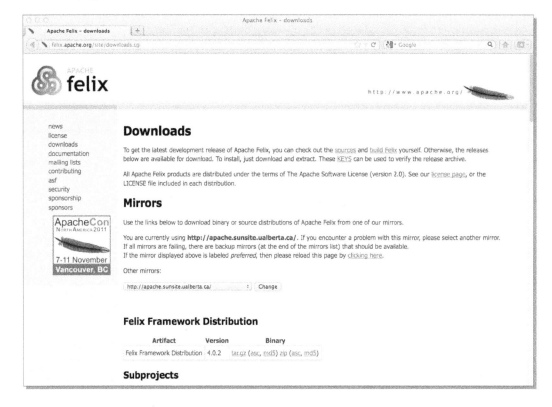

Alternatively, you can also get an OSGi core as a compressed package from `http://download.eclipse.org/equinox`. The following screenshot shows the Eclipse Equinox download page:

## Step 3 – starting up an OSGi core directly

Starting the OSGi framework is as simple as executing the following command:

```
$java -jar bin/felix.jar
```

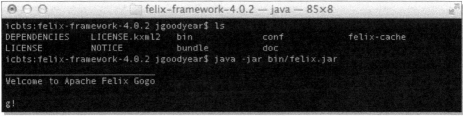

Apache Felix Gogo shell

This will start the Apache Felix Gogo shell, a shell for interacting with the OSGi environment. Type help to see a list of available commands. To exit the shell, press *Ctrl + C*.

## Step 4 – downloading Apache Karaf

Using a bare OSGi framework can be an unwieldy experience for a first time OSGi developer. As such, we encourage new users to try an OSGi environment such as Apache Karaf or Eclipse Virgo. Apache Karaf, by default, uses Apache Felix as it is an OSGi framework while Eclipse Virgo uses Eclipse Equinox. Both runtime containers provide an enhanced experience when working with OSGi environments. For more information on Eclipse Equinox please visit
`http://www.eclipse.org/equinox/`.

### What does using Apache Karaf and Maven provide us with?

Apache Karaf is a full OSGi environment, which provides an enriched out-of-the-box experience to users and developers alike. Apache Maven provides a provisioning mechanism that simplifies the process of obtaining and configuring dependencies required for your OSGi projects. A few highlights of using Apache Karaf include: Hot Deployment of OSGi bundles, Dynamic Configuration via OSGi's ConfigurationAdmin service, a centralized logging system, built-in provisioning mechanisms to simplify gathering resources, native OS integration, an extensible shell console, remote access, security framework, and OSGi instance management, among other great features!

Apache Karaf Download Page

## Step 5 – starting Apache Karaf

Starting Apache Karaf is as simple as executing the Karaf start script in the `bin` folder of your Karaf distribution. In our opinion, Apache Karaf's shell is easier to use than diving straight into writing a similar infrastructure for deployment using a bare OSGi runtime. You get a tab for completion of commands, a greatly expanded repertoire of commands and tooling that will help you develop, monitor, and deploy your projects. Note here that Apache Karaf can be installed as a system service, allowing the OSGi container to be started and stopped as any other service (See Apache Karaf documentation for details).

Change the directory to Karaf's `bin` folder and execute the Karaf script to start the environment as follows:

**$karaf[.bat]**

Apache Karaf interactive shell

## Step 6 – obtaining the BND tool (Maven Bundle plugin)

Building OSGi bundles is a relatively straightforward operation consisting of adding OSGi headers to your Java Archive's Manifest file. Our recommendation, however, is to use tools to handle generating the file entries. The easiest way to do this is to use the Maven Bundle plugin.

Acquiring the plugin can be accomplished by adding the following to your plugin repositories section of your Maven project:

```
<dependency>
    <groupId>org.apache.felix</groupId>
    <artifactId>maven-bundle-plugin</artifactId>
    <version>${felix.plugin.version}</version>
    <!-- <scope>provided|compile|test</scope> -->
</dependency>
```

Note that Maven properties are accessed using `${property.name}`, and they are defined in a property element as `<properties><property.name></property.name></properties>`.

Maven provides several scopes; these are optional. For container providing dependencies you want to use the scope provided. Other commonly used scopes are `compile` and `test`.

Once you've added the plugin dependency you can invoke the plugin by configuring its execution. We'll explore the BND tool's use in the sections that follow.

## Step 7 – obtaining Blueprint

**Blueprint** is a dependency injection framework for OSGi, its job is to handle the wiring of JavaBeans, and instantiation and life cycle of an application. Blueprint also helps with the dynamic nature of OSGi where services can come and go at any time. Blueprint is expressed as an XML file that defines and describes how the various components are assembled together, instantiated, and wired together to build an executing module.

In our demo code, Blueprint will be expressed as a top-level element:

```
<?xml version="1.0" encoding="UTF-8"?>
<blueprint xmlns="http://www.osgi.org/xmlns/blueprint/v1.0.0">
</blueprint>
```

The namespace indicates that the document conforms to Blueprint's Version 1.0.0, the schema of which can be viewed at `http://www.osgi.org/xmlns/blueprint/v1.0.0/blueprint.xsd`.

## Step 8 – obtaining Pax Exam

In a container, testing your OSGi applications is easy—just grab Pax Exam! This tool allows you to launch an OSGi framework, build bundles as defined in your test cases, and inject them into the container. Multiple testing strategies are available, allowing you to thoroughly validate your application.

To pick up Pax Exam for your testing, add the following dependency to your Maven project's object model file:

```
<dependency>
    <groupId>org.ops4j.pax.exam</groupId>
    <artifactId>pax-exam</artifactId>
    <version>${pax.exam.version}</version>
</dependency>
```

We'll explore using Pax Exam in the sections that follow.

## And that's it!!

By this point, you should have a working installation of OSGI (preferably Apache Karaf) and you're free to play around and discover more about it.

# Quick start – your first OSGi bundles

OSGi bundles are the cornerstones of a modular OSGi application. In this section we'll guide you through building your first example application. This application consists of a set of Apache Maven modules that'll generate, compile, and test your application code. The whole set of modules is prefabricated for your convenience so that you can spend time on analyzing and modifying the project to suit your specific needs.

All of the source code for the examples is located at GitHub, a free git hosting provider. The following screenshot shows the OSGi Starter GitHub project page. To build the sources you'll need git to integrate and download the source (you can download the sources as a ZIP file as well from `https://github.com/seijoed/osgi-starter/zipball/master`), and Apache Maven to actually compile the projects.

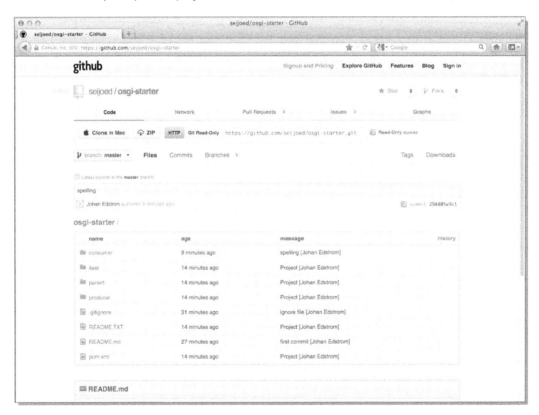

To obtain a copy of the code you may perform a git clone of the project.

```
● ○ ○                     🗀 demo — bash — 90×9                          ↖↗
icbts:demo jgoodyear$ git clone https://github.com/seijoed/osgi-starter.git
Cloning into 'osgi-starter'...
remote: Counting objects: 58, done.
remote: Compressing objects: 100% (30/30), done.
remote: Total 58 (delta 6), reused 54 (delta 2)
Unpacking objects: 100% (58/58), done.
icbts:demo jgoodyear$
```

The projects utilize Apache Maven and the Apache Felix plugins; this will provide us with quick and easy tooling integration, a single build command, as well as integrated testing of all of the projects.

Start by navigating to the GitHub URL containing the demonstration code (`https://github.com/seijoed/osgi-starter`), and then clone the sources (`https://github.com/seijoed/osgi-starter.git`) to a local directory. Make sure that you have Apache Maven set up correctly and on the PATH of your shell or command-line window.

## Step 1 – what do I need?

For the OSGi tutorial you'll need all of the components downloaded in the previous section as well as Apache Maven and a Java JDK. Once you have downloaded the project you'll have a structure consisting of a consumer, producer, itest, and parent project.

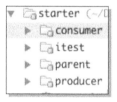

The parent project is used to allow for building properties as well as Apache Maven plugin inheritance; the itests contain the integration tests for the projects. This allows you to have a continuous integration cycle while writing your modules. It also prevents the necessity of needing to have a complete OSGi container running at all times during the development cycle.

To build the project invoke the following command:

```
%> mvn install
```

Each module will in turn be compiled with artifacts placed into your local Maven repository. Note that during the build you will observe unit tests being performed and reported upon; more on this will be discussed shortly. The following screenshot shows a successful build of the application:

```
○ ○ ○                    🗀 osgi-starter — bash — 100×27
Tests run: 2, Failures: 0, Errors: 0, Skipped: 0

[INFO]
[INFO] --- maven-jar-plugin:2.3.1:jar (default-jar) @ itest ---
[INFO] Building jar: /x4/demo/osgi-starter/itest/target/itest-1.0.jar
[INFO]
[INFO] --- maven-install-plugin:2.3.1:install (default-install) @ itest ---
[INFO] Installing /x4/demo/osgi-starter/itest/target/itest-1.0.jar to /Users/jgoodyear/.m2/repositor
y/starter/itest/1.0/itest-1.0.jar
[INFO] Installing /x4/demo/osgi-starter/itest/pom.xml to /Users/jgoodyear/.m2/repository/starter/ite
st/1.0/itest-1.0.pom
[INFO] ------------------------------------------------------------------------
[INFO] Reactor Summary:
[INFO]
[INFO] starter ........................................... SUCCESS [0.110s]
[INFO] parent ............................................ SUCCESS [0.004s]
[INFO] producer .......................................... SUCCESS [1.999s]
[INFO] consumer .......................................... SUCCESS [0.744s]
[INFO] itest ............................................. SUCCESS [6.616s]
[INFO] ------------------------------------------------------------------------
[INFO] BUILD SUCCESS
[INFO] ------------------------------------------------------------------------
[INFO] Total time: 10.858s
[INFO] Finished at: Sun Aug 19 16:18:13 NDT 2012
[INFO] Final Memory: 22M/81M
[INFO] ------------------------------------------------------------------------
icbts:osgi-starter jgoodyear$
```

## Step 2 – analyzing the producer

The producer module contains a few key components, one of them being the Maven bundle plugin (illustrated in the following screenshot) that exports the packages containing the interfaces and hides the implementation of exported API components. This allows for a complete separation of concerns.

```xml
<plugins>
  <plugin>
    <groupId>org.apache.felix</groupId>
    <artifactId>maven-bundle-plugin</artifactId>
    <extensions>true</extensions>
    <configuration>
      <instructions>
        <Export-Package>com.packt.osgi.starter.producer</Export-Package>
        <Private-Package>com.packt.osgi.starter.producer.impl</Private-Package>
        <Bundle-Activator>com.packt.osgi.starter.producer.impl.ProducerActivator</Bundle-Activator>
      </instructions>
    </configuration>
  </plugin>
</plugins>
```

The plugin will build the META-INF/MANIFEST.MF file for us (thereby saving us from having to manually populate the bundle headers that make the produced JAR an OSGi bundle), exporting all classes in the package com.packt.osgi.starter.producer while hiding everything in the impl package. We do this in order to hide from the unnecessary framework packages, otherwise we'd have to import what we are exporting. The impl package also contains Bundle-Activator. This activator is going to take part in the OSGi life cycle, implementing org.osgi.framework.BundleActivator that allows us to mark a class as executable by the OSGi framework. When the bundle transitions from resolution and has satisfied imports and exports as per the MANIFEST.MF file this class will be called from the framework and activated.

```
Manifest-Version: 1.0
Bnd-LastModified: 1342372664594
Build-Jdk: 1.6.0_33
Built-By: joed
Bundle-Activator: com.packt.osgi.starter.producer.impl.ProducerActivator
Bundle-ManifestVersion: 2
Bundle-Name: producer
Bundle-SymbolicName: starter.producer
Bundle-Version: 1.0.0
Created-By: Apache Maven Bundle Plugin
Export-Package: com.packt.osgi.starter.producer;version="1.0.0"
Import-Package: com.packt.osgi.starter.producer,org.osgi.framework;version="[1.5,2)"
Tool: Bnd-1.50.0
```

This file tells the OSGi container all it needs to know about the JAR; it specifies starting parameters, imports, what we have asked to export, and symbolic information containing build tool, builder, and versioning information. The following screenshot shows the **BundleActivator** interface for the producer bundle:

```
public class ProducerActivator implements BundleActivator {

    RequestResponseApi requestResponse = new RequestResponseService();
    ServiceRegistration registration;

    public void start(BundleContext bundleContext) throws Exception {
        //Register the service with the container.
        //Register the interface, implementation and possible properties
        registration = bundleContext.registerService(RequestResponseApi.class.getName(), requestResponse, null);
    }

    public void stop(BundleContext bundleContext) throws Exception {
        //When we stop, clean up the references.
        registration.unregister();
    }
}
```

The Service registration for this bundle is one single line. Utilizing `org.osgi.framework.BundleContext` (the bundle's execution context) we register a service for our interface. It allows the bundle to interact with the environment interface. The context gives you access to the OSGi service registry as well as resolution of other bundles if so desired. There are several other interfaces besides `BundleActivator` that you can implement to get event, logging, container, and bundle information.

**Apache Karaf command**

Look through some of the APIs for `org.osgi.framework.BundleContext` and you'll see what you can do with a running bundle!

To quickly install and start the producer bundle in Karaf, issue the `osgi:install` command (`bundle:install -s` on Karaf 3.x). The short hand `install -s` tells Karaf to resolve and start the bundle. Note that the same command will work on Linux, Unix, or Windows (no additional configuration required) as follows:

```
karaf@root> install -s mvn:com.packt.osgi.
starter/1.0.0/producer
```

After the bundle has been deployed to Apache Karaf it will show up in the console as an Active and running bundle. We can see the bundle state, ID, name, and if it contains a Blueprint context.

```
START LEVEL 100 , List Threshold: 50
   ID    State            Blueprint       Level   Name
[  50] [Active      ] [                ] [   80] producer (1.0.0)
```

```
producer (50) provides:
----------------------
objectClass = com.packt.osgi.starter.producer.RequestResponseApi
service.id = 184
```

Since we also had `BundleActivator` that registered a service, we can list the service registry to ensure that our service has been registered correctly. Our producer bundle is now activated; the service is registered and ready for subscription.

Congratulations, you have just deployed your first piece of modular software!

# Step 3 – analyzing the consumer

The consumer is built from two Java classes and a deployment file for Aries Blueprint. Blueprint being an inversion of control and dependency injection framework for OSGi, Blueprint allows you to write simple Java beans, inject services and references. The following screenshot shows the relevant package structure for the Consumer in Maven format, showing classes and resources in the correct locations for a bundle deployment:

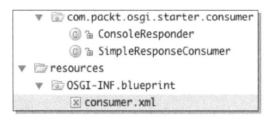

Once the blueprint file is deployed, a blueprint extender will parse it, and your bundle will be handed a recipe to deploy that contains the correct wiring. We utilize it here to consume the service from the producer; the blueprint container will handle the service subscription and related error handling for us. Aries Blueprint instantiates a blueprint container for us. According to the blueprint.xml configuration file, it also will take the reference, that is our service subscription, and inject it as a field in SimpleResponseConsumer.

```xml
<?xml version="1.0" encoding="UTF-8" standalone="no"?>
<blueprint xmlns="http://www.osgi.org/xmlns/blueprint/v1.0.0"
        xmlns:xsi="http://www.w3.org/2001/XMLSchema-instance"
        xsi:schemaLocation="http://www.osgi.org/xmlns/blueprint/v1.0.0
        http://www.osgi.org/xmlns/blueprint/v1.0.0/blueprint.xsd">

    <!-- This context will be scanned and the service references injected to our bean -->
    <bean id="consumer" class="com.packt.osgi.starter.consumer.SimpleResponseConsumer" init-method="init">
      <property name="request" ref="responder"/>
    </bean>

    <!-- OSGi service reference -->
    <reference id="responder" interface="com.packt.osgi.starter.producer.RequestResponseApi"/>
```

The consumer class contains a simple java.util.Timer that will utilize the service on a schedule.

**Apache Karaf command**

To quickly install and start the consumer bundle in Karaf, issue the osgi:install command (bundle:install –s on Karaf 3.x) as follows:

karaf@root> install –s mvn:com.packt.osgi. starter/1.0.0/consumer

Once the consumer is deployed, it will start the bundle and then create a Blueprint container. Aries, being a set of bundles that provide OSGi development tools (we will discuss Blueprint more in depth in a later section), creates the Blueprint container. The container will activate our consumer class. The consumer then instantiates a timer and passes in a reference to the service into `TimerTask` (`TimerTasks` are used to schedule an action to occur once, or repeatedly).

```
START LEVEL 100 , List Threshold: 50
    ID    State            Blueprint      Level  Name
[  50] [Active        ] [              ] [   80] producer (1.0.0)
[  51] [Active        ] [Created       ] [   80] consumer (1.0.0)
```

Once this is activated, you'll see your console screen starting to fill up with service requests, as follows:

```
You called the service with Time is 1343516178956
You called the service with Time is 1343516183956
You called the service with Time is 1343516188955
```

These requests are from a full life cycle project. We have our producer deployed, running, and providing a service. The consumer bundle is resolved, loaded, and instantiated by Apache Aries Blueprint; the proxy from the Blueprint framework consumes the service and our Java classes are now able to invoke methods until we stop execution.

## Step 4 – testing

Since we are building this demo system OSGi, a technology built around runtime, we'll illustrate this in the testing phase with an integration test. Integration tests are natural extensions of regular unit tests where we also involve the necessary components to execute our code in the test bed. In the code examples, we use a framework called Pax Exam combined with Junit to execute, mark, and define our test suite. We also rely on a new plugin; this plugin is going to write out dependency information for us so that the Pax Exam execution environment can re-use this information and allow us to simplify our test configurations.

```
<build>
  <plugins>
    <!-- generate dependencies versions -->
    <plugin>
      <groupId>org.apache.servicemix.tooling</groupId>
      <artifactId>depends-maven-plugin</artifactId>
      <executions>
        <execution>
          <id>generate-depends-file</id>
          <goals>
            <goal>generate-depends-file</goal>
          </goals>
        </execution>
      </executions>
    </plugin>
  </plugins>
</build>
```

Note that you can configure the use of a specific version of the plugin using the tags
`<version></version>`.

We also add a set of dependencies in our Apache Maven pom file; these contain Pax Exam
artifacts, an execution model as well as the projects we wish to test. Pax Exam allows us to
annotate a configure model. In this model, we specify all of the various bundles that we need
to load for a complete test cycle.

Loading these, we re-use the Apache Maven plugin; it enables us to let Pax Exam figure out
the right dependency versions from the build environment. This will lead to less manual work
when you are upgrading versions or modifying the tests.

```
@Configuration
public Option[] config() {
    Option[] options = combine(options(mavenBundle("org.osgi", "org.osgi.compendium"),
        mavenBundle("asm", "asm-all"),
        mavenBundle("org.apache.aries", "org.apache.aries.util").versionAsInProject(),
        mavenBundle("org.apache.aries.blueprint", "org.apache.aries.blueprint").versionAsInProject(),
        mavenBundle("org.apache.aries.proxy", "org.apache.aries.proxy").versionAsInProject(),
        mavenBundle("asm","asm-all"),

        junitBundles(), mavenBundle("starter", "producer").versionAsInProject(),
        mavenBundle("starter", "consumer").versionAsInProject()));

    return options;
}
```

We also configure a Junit runner and a Pax Exam reactor strategy for the execution of our test.
Both of these are annotations that will provide test behavior; the first tells Junit how to run our
tests and the second tells Pax Exam what execution strategy we want to utilize.

```
@RunWith(JUnit4TestRunner.class)
@ExamReactorStrategy(value = AllConfinedStagedReactorFactory.class)
```

Once we run this test, either from the command line via an mvn test or from within an IDE, we will see Pax Exam starting an OSGi container for us, loading the necessary bundles, loading our bundles, and lastly our Junit test will be executed.

The test-code that does all of the heavy lifting is shown in the following screenshot:

```
@Test
public void testServiceRegistration() {
    assertNotNull(request);
    assertTrue("You called the service with ding".equals(request.getResponse("ding")));
}
```

This is a very simple little test suite that does quite a few things. We rely on a few niceties of Pax Exam, so we let Pax Exam inject our service for us. Then we make sure that the service is valid and not null, and lastly we actually exercise the service with a predictable request where we can anticipate the response. Having reached this far in the tests, we know that we have accomplished quite a few things; they are as follows:

- ✦ Our bundles are correct with regards to imports and exports
- ✦ We know that Aries Blueprint is loading our context correctly
- ✦ We know that we are correctly registering a service
- ✦ We know that we correctly and predictably can use the service
- ✦ We know that our APIs are correctly implemented

Comparing the two tests in the test suite, the `ProducerAndConsumerTest` is vastly more complicated, primarily due to external dependencies since the consumer is using Apache Aries Blueprint. This helps to illustrate the point for modularity since we can clearly show that the more things we add to a bundle, the likelihood of us using more technologies will grow, sometimes exponentially.

Our test bundles, in all fairness, are not that complicated though, so it isn't much of an issue for this exercise, but the argument being made is that decoupled, simple, and predictable code is going to be far simpler to test. This will, in particular, hold true for systems that introduce concurrency and are needed to scale.

To illustrate what we really have deployed, we'll introduce the following UML diagram containing all of the existing deployments we have done against this source:

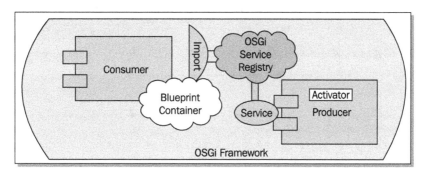

The preceding diagram is using OSGi UML symbols to describe the entire example project. Starting from the left, we have a **Consumer** bundle (represented using a component icon); it is utilizing **Blueprint Container** to import services from **OSGi Service Registry** (the stylistic details vary; however, imports are depicted as a receptacle, while exports are depicted as a matching shape to plug in to the import). **Blueprint Container** is an additional API component that has a slightly different life cycle from the native OSGi one, hence it is clearly broken out and illustrated as a separate container. The major life cycle difference is that since **Blueprint Container** is more or less custom code executing in a bundle, that bundle technically can be started with a failed Blueprint context.

At the other end, we have our OSGi native **Producer** bundle (also represented using a component icon). This bundle contains nothing but pure framework code, thus it exports to and communicates directly with **OSGi Service Registry** (shown in the following diagram). We have used both approaches in the examples. Blueprint is a dependency injection and inversion of control framework modeled closely to the Spring Framework. It is a development style that has become very popular and successful in the Java world as it allows you to quickly configure rather complex applications from very simple building blocks. If you are writing more container or framework-oriented code, it is likely that you'll look more at `BundleActivators` and pure OSGi code; the choice is left to the reader!

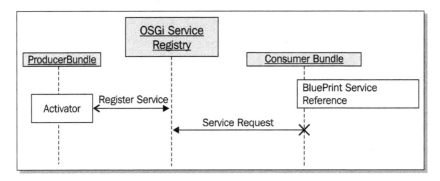

Note that the solid arrow represents invoking and the line arrow represents return in the preceding diagram.

Another common way of describing bundles and their tasks is to use sequence diagrams; these diagrams depict object interactions in a time sequence. Combining a sequence diagram with a high-level abstract UML diagram will provide you with ample documentation of what your bundles are actually doing. We are not intending to provide UML education, so see these diagrams as simplified documentation intended to be at a fairly high level, and describing exactly what we have in our bundles and deployable units.

We start from left to right; **ProducerBundle** is resolved, starts, and then contacts **OSGi Service Registry** to register a service. Once completed, it will wait until a service subscription request is initiated. The subscription request is performed by **ConsumerBundle**, this bundle will resolve dependencies, start, and the extender pattern (this pattern will be explained in a later section) from the blueprint provider will kick in and help us initiate the Blueprint context file. Once the Blueprint recipe is resolved and composed, it will instantiate our classes and communicate with the service registry to start its subscription. If the subscription is unavailable, by default, the Blueprint container will wait with a configurable timeout until a service is registered. This is one of the reasons that frameworks like Blueprint are popular; they allow you to focus on your business code instead of error handling and boilerplate code.

# Top five features you'll want to know about

As you start to use OSGi, you will realize that there are a wide variety of things that you can do with it. This section will teach you all about the most commonly performed tasks and most commonly used features, as follows:

+ OSGi headers
+ OSGi life cycle
+ OSGi core services
+ OSGi compendium services
+ OSGi modular patterns

## 1 – OSGi headers

We have so far touched on OSGi headers, the special entries found in Java Archive Manifest files that make a JAR into a bundle. There exists a large collection of these headers, and different organizations add additional ones to assist in specific application domains. As a quick reference guide, we have prepared a table of OSGi headers and their purpose.

| Header | Purpose |
| --- | --- |
| `Bundle-ActivationPolicy` | This tells runtime if the bundle should be loaded lazily, meaning start is not called until the first access of the class occurs. |
| `Bundle-Activator` | It specifies the class implementing the `org.osgi.framework.BundleActivator` interface. |
| `Bundle-Category` | A comma-separated list of category names. |
| `Bundle-Classpath` | This is a manual control of where to load classes from within the bundle. The default is "." or the root of the bundle; however, one may specify embedded jars into the classpath. |
| `Bundle-ContactAddress` | This specifies where to find more information on the bundle. Typically a website URL, organization, or project maintainer. |
| `Bundle-Copyright` | Indicates copyright holder of the bundle. |
| `Bundle-Description` | A brief text description of the bundle's purpose. |
| `Bundle-DocURL` | URL to find more information in a bundle. |

| Header | Purpose |
| --- | --- |
| Bundle-Icon | A list of icon URLs that can be used to represent the bundle. Icon files may be internal to the bundle or an absolute web address. No specific format is required. |
| Bundle-License | This describes which license(s) the bundle is available under. |
| Bundle-Localization | This references a set of property files, which may be used to localize the bundle. It is typically used for language support, currency, and units of measurement. |
| Bundle-ManifestVersion | This is an optional header, and defaults to Version 1. As of OSGi R4, the value 2 was introduced. Most bundles have Version 2 specified. |
| Bundle-Name | Text identifier for the bundle. |
| Bundle-NativeCode | This is used to provide information about native libraries that should be loaded by the bundle. |
| Bundle-RequiredExecution Environment | This is a list of execution environments (JVM versions) that must be present for the bundle to be installed. |
| Bundle-SymbolicName | Along with Bundle-Version, these headers are used to uniquely identify a bundle at runtime. This header is mandatory. |
| Bundle-UpdateLocation | This indicates where the bundle should look for updates to the OSGi runtime bundle.update() call. |
| Bundle-Vendor | This is the vendor of the bundle. |
| Bundle-Version | This is the version of the bundle in the Major.Minor.Micro.Qualifier format. The first three fields are numeric, while the qualifier can be any text value. |
| DynamicImport-Package | Wires to packages that may not be known in advance. Using this feature is expensive as the framework must search all exported packages instead of using a calculation. |
| Embed-Dependency | This acts as a macro to include resources and updates the Bundle-Classpath header to pick up these resources at runtime. |
| Export-Package | This makes a comma-separated list of packages available to other bundles. |

| Header | Purpose |
| --- | --- |
| Export-Service | Deprecated – formerly used to make static exports, services are now consumed dynamically. |
| Fragment-Host | This identifies the parent bundle this fragment should attach to. |
| Import-Package | This bundle's package level dependencies. At runtime, the OSGi framework will be the bundle to any compatible bundle that provides the required package. |
| Import-Service | Deprecated – formerly used to make static imports, services are now consumed dynamically. |
| Include-Resource | BND tool header – copies resource into JAR. |
| Private-Package | BND tool header – specifies packages that are not exported. |
| Provide-Capability | This is part of the generic requirements/capabilities model for bundle wiring. Export package statements are translated into capabilities. |
| Require-Bundle | This declares a dependency with a bundle-symbolic name instead of a package name. Import-Package is the preferred mechanism. |
| Require-Capability | Bundle requires capabilities provided by another bundle. The imported package and required bundle are translated into requirements, but they can be anything we want as a requirement. |

While the preceding table is helpful in quickly understanding some of the most commonly seen headers in the core specification, out of which we have listed a few custom headers, several more exist for various tools such as BND, Eclipse, and Spring. We feel that we should look a little closer at Bundle-SymbolicName, Bundle-Version, Import-Package, and Export-Package.

**Apache Karaf command**

To view headers of installed bundles quickly, issue the osgi:headers (bundle:headers on Karaf 3.x) command as follows:

```
karaf@root> osgi:headers BundleID
```

## Bundle-SymbolicName

The `SymbolicName` of a bundle is the only mandatory header that an OSGi bundle must contain. This header supports a directive to indicate if the bundle should be treated as a singleton, or that only one bundle of this name should exist in the framework:

```
Bundle-SymbolicName: com.packt.osgi.starter;singleton:=true
```

 The singleton directive lets the OSGi environment know that there should only be one bundle in the system with this name at the same time.

## Bundle-Version

Along with `Bundle-SymbolicName`, this attribute uniquely identifies a bundle in the framework. Additional attention needs to be paid to OSGi versioning as the OSGi environment will pay strict attention to version requirements as defined by the bundle's import and export packages.

The generally adhered practice for versioning is as follows:

```
Major.Minor.Micro.Qualifier
```

### Major

A major number indicates incompatibilities in bundle use between versions, that is, incompatible changes in APIs.

### Minor

A minor number indicates that this is a backward compatible build, and users should be safe updating to a higher version (of course you should always verify through testing). However, if the version applies to an API package, implementers of the package will not work. For instance, adding a method to an API is a minor version change.

### Micro

A micro version update indicates that an internal change has occurred, but it does not alter its APIs. Normally, this is used when bug fixes are made to the bundle.

### Qualifier

A qualifier is used to indicate small internal changes, or to communicate to the users' bundle status, that is, a milestone build.

```
Bundle-Version: 1.0.0.milestone1
```

```
Bundle-Version: 1.0.0.SNAPSHOT
```

# Import-Package

A bundle declares its dependencies through this header. The semantics surrounding the version attribute merits additional attention; the use of (' and ') denotes exclusive values, and [' and '] denotes inclusive values. These braces are used to denote version ranges. There are five cases we must examine:

### Inclusive Minimum, Exclusive Maximum:

The version is denoted with " [minimum, maximum) ", which translates to "wire to package with at least minimum version, up to but not including the maximum version". This version range is commonly seen when your wiring bundles to us up to the next major version of a library.

```
Import-Package: com.packt.some.package;version="[1.2.3, 2.0.0)"
```

### Inclusive Minimum, Inclusive Maximum:

The version is denoted with " [minimum, maximum] ", which translates to "wire to package with at least minimum version, up to and including the maximum version".

Typically, these ranges are used when bundle compatibility is known for a very specific set of releases.

```
Import-Package: com.packt.some.package;version="[1.2.3, 1.2.99]"
```

### Exclusive Minimum, Exclusive Maximum:

The version is denoted with " (minimum, maximum) ", which translates to "wire to package higher than the minimum version, up to but not including the maximum version."

```
Import-Package: com.packt.some.package;version="(1.2.3, 2.0.0)"
```

Note that the range [1.2.4, 2.0.0) may be more practical to use.

### Exclusive Minimum, Inclusive Maximum:

The version is denoted with " (minimum, maximum] ", which translates to "wire to package higher than the minimum version, up to and including the maximum version".

```
Import-Package: com.packt.some.package;version="(1.2.3, 2.0.0]"
```

### Inclusive Minimum:

The version is denoted with "minimum", which translates to "wire to package with at least minimum version". This particular notation can be a source of confusion as the framework will wire the highest version available of the package requested. It's a good practice to always state a version range to avoid issues from future packages not being compatible with your bundle.

```
Import-Package: com.packt.some.package;version="1.2.3"
```

> **Apache Karaf command**
>
>
>
> To view which bundles are providing packages to your bundle imports, issue the `dev:show-tree` (`bundle:tree-show` on Karaf 3.x) command, as follows:
>
> `karaf@root> dev:show-tree BundleID`

## Export-Package

This header is used to tell the framework if any packages are being provided by this bundle to the environment. Package names should be fully qualified and include a version attribute. When the version attribute is not provided, the version is defaulted to `0.0.0`.

`Export-Package: com.packt.util, com.packt.osgi;version="1.0"`

Now that we have a deeper understanding of bundles, let's look closer at their life cycle.

## 2 – OSGi life cycle

We have described OSGi applications as living entities; by this we mean that these applications appear to evolve as the life cycles of their constituent bundles are lived. The life cycle layer facilitates this functionality.

OSGi bundles are dynamically installed, resolved, started, updated, stopped, and uninstalled. The framework enforces the transitions between states, one cannot directly install a bundle and jump to an Active state without first passing through the resolved and starting states. The transitions between each state are illustrated in the following figure:

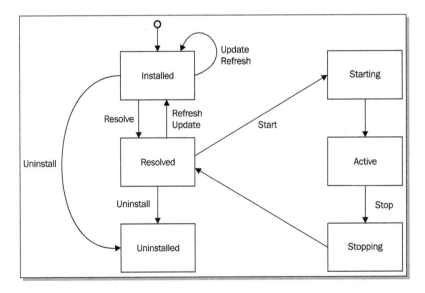

## Installed

Bundles came into existence in an OSGi framework in the installed state. A bundle in this state cannot be immediately started, as the preceding diagram depicts that there is no direct transition from the installed state to the starting state. An installed bundle is also not active. There are three possible transitions: the bundle may become resolved, uninstalled, or refreshed.

**Apache Karaf command**

To install a bundle in Karaf, issue the `osgi:install` (`bundle:install` on Karaf 3.x) command, as follows:

`karaf@root> osgi:install URLs`

Having a bundle installed to the OSGi framework does not mean it is ready to be used; next we must resolve its dependencies.

## Resolved

Entering the resolved state requires the framework to ensure that all the dependencies of a bundle have been met. Upon having its dependencies ensured, the bundle is now a candidate to be transitioned to the starting state. A resolved bundle may be refreshed, transitioning the bundle back to the installed state. A resolved bundle may also be transitioned to the uninstalled state. A resolved bundle is not active; however, it is ready to be activated.

**Apache Karaf command**

To resolve an installed bundle in Karaf, issue the `osgi:resolve` (`bundle:resolve` on Karaf 3.x) command, as follows:

`karaf@root> osgi:resolve BundleID`

## Starting

A resolved bundle may be started. The starting state is transitory; the framework is initializing the resolved bundle into a running active state. In fact, the transition from the starting to active state is implicit.

**Apache Karaf command**

To start a resolved bundle in Karaf, issue the `osgi:start` (`bundle:start` on Karaf 3.x) command, as follows:

`karaf@root> osgi:start BundleID`

## Active

The bundle is fully resolved, providing and consuming services in the OSGi environment. To perform any more transitions on an active bundle, it must first be stopped.

## Updating

Bundle updates occur when the framework is instructed to re-evaluate a bundle's dependencies; this action is synonymous with refreshing a bundle. When this action occurs, all of the wiring to and from the bundle is broken, so care must be taken before refreshing to avoid starting a bundle storm (one bundle refreshing causes a domino effect of other bundles refreshing).

**Apache Karaf command**

To update a bundle in Karaf, issue the `osgi:update` (`bundle:update` on Karaf 3.x) command, as follows:

```
karaf@root> osgi:update BundleID [location]
```

The `location` option allows you to update the bundle via its predefined updated location or to specify a new location to find bundle updates.

## Stopping

Stopping a bundle transitions it from the active to the resolved state. The bundle can be restarted while it remains in the resolved state.

**Apache Karaf command**

To stop an active bundle in Karaf, issue the `osgi:stop` (`bundle:stop` on Karaf 3.x) command, as follows:

```
karaf@root> osgi:stop BundleID
```

## Uninstalled

Uninstalling a bundle transitions an installed or resolved bundle out of the OSGi environment; however, the bundle is not removed from the environment! Why is this? While the bundle is no longer available for use, references to the bundle may still exist and used for introspection.

To help leverage these states in your bundles, the OSGi specification provides a hook into your bundle state via the `Activator` interface.

**Apache Karaf command**

To uninstall a bundle in Karaf, issue the `osgi:uninstall` (`bundle:uninstall` on Karaf 3.x) command, as follows:

```
karaf@root> osgi:uninstall BundleID
```

# BundleActivator

A bundle may optionally declare an `Activator` class implementing the `org.osgi.framework.BundleActivator` interface. This class must be referenced in the bundle manifest file via the `BundleActivator` header. Implementing the activator allows the bundle developer to specify actions to be performed upon starting or stopping a bundle. Generally, such operations include gaining access to or freeing resources, and registering and unregistering services.

The entry in `manifest.mf` will appear as follows:

```
Bundle-Activator: com.packt.osgi.starter.sample.Activator
```

When building with `maven-bundle-plugin`, the following configuration instruction is added:

```
<Bundle-Activator>
com.packt.osgi.starter.sample.Activator
</Bundle-Activator>
```

The process can be seen in the following screenshot:

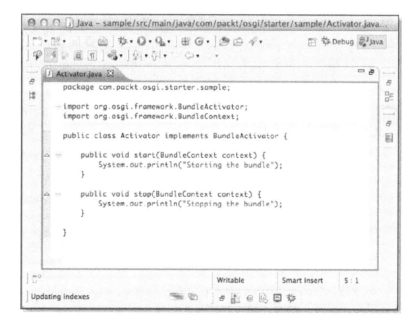

# 3 – OSGi core services

In this section we'll review the core OSGi services. The published specification for Rev 4.2 of the OSGi Framework is 332 pages long. As such, we've highly condensed the material in this section. To read the entire specification please visit `http://www.osgi.org/Download/Release4V42`.

| OSGi Core Service | Purpose |
| --- | --- |
| Conditional Permission Admin | The OSGi framework specification contains both the Permission Admin and the Conditional Permission Admin that supersedes the former one. |
| | You can also specify a Java policy file for security. |
| | The recommended usage is that of the Conditional Permission Admin; it is newer and more powerful. |
| | Conditional Permission Admin service extends the Permission Admin service with permissions that can apply when certain conditions are either true or false at the time the permission is checked. These conditions determine the selection of the bundles to which the permissions apply. Permissions are activated immediately after they are set. |
| Package Admin | A framework service allows bundle programmers to inspect the packages exported in the framework and eagerly update or uninstall bundles. |
| Permission Admin | The Permission Admin service enables the OSGi framework management agent to administer the permissions of a specific bundle and to provide defaults for all bundles. A bundle can have a single set of permissions that are used to verify that it is authorized to execute privileged code. You can dynamically manipulate permissions by changing policies on the fly and by adding new policies for newly installed components. Policy files are used to control what bundles can do. |
| Start Level | The core specification controls for start levels are as follows: |
| | ✦ The beginning start level of the OSGi framework |
| | ✦ Can modify the active start level of the framework |
| | ✦ Can be used to assign a specific start level to a bundle |
| | ✦ Can set the initial start level for newly installed bundles |

| OSGi Core Service | Purpose |
| --- | --- |
| Service hooks | The OSGi service hooks are the framework primitives for service interactions; those primitives are as follows:<br><br>✦ Register a service (Publish)<br><br>✦ Find services (Find)<br><br>✦ Get a service (Bind)<br><br>✦ Listen for service events |
| URL Handlers | The URL Handlers service extends the standard Java URL stream and content handler mechanism to work in an OSGi environment.<br><br>The way that the built-in URL protocol and content handlers are discovered is by probing packages for the appropriate classes to handle the protocol/content.<br><br>If someone tries to create a URL for the HTTP protocol, then the class to handle the protocol will be `sun.net.www.protocol.http.Handler` as it is registered by default from a Sun JVM. |

The preceding table provides a concise introduction to the framework services. Our experience in using OSGi environments, however, encourages us to further explore Service hooks as an area that requires more attention.

## Service Hooks

These Service Hooks are not intended for regular bundle developers, they are there to facilitate things like distributed OSGi. Service Hooks are not to be confused with the service engine publish, find, and bind methods.

A common usage scenario for a Service Hook is in an OSGi system where all communication is normally tunneled through services; this makes it a very interesting place for a handler to intercept the service communications. The hooks allow you to install handlers that can help facilitate things like proxying, security, authentication, and other functions more or less like interceptors.

This behavior will be completely transparent to the consumer of the service that will only be interacting with the OSGi service registry.

To proxy an existing service for a specific bundle, we would be required to perform the following steps:

1. Hide the existing service X.
2. Register a proxy X with the same properties of X.

Properties here are very simple; we really are only talking about the same interface and potential filters necessary. When these criteria are met, a proxy can pose as the original service and add additional work to the registration.

## 4 – OSGi Compendium Services

In attempting to keep our view of OSGi simple, we've tried to keep our review to the core OSGi specification; however, this leaves out the richness found in the OSGi compendium. All of these additional services will allow you to enhance the bundle life cycle, control, and manage various things such as dependency injection, configuration metadata, user administration, and so on. To discover these services more in detail, please visit `http://www.osgi.org/Download/Release4V42`.

| OSGi Compendium Service | Purpose |
| --- | --- |
| Application Admin | Application manager abstraction is used to manage application types. |
| Blueprint Container | This is a dependency injection framework based on the Spring DM programming model. It has been designed to handle OSGi's dynamic environment where services come and go. |
| Configuration Admin | This is used for handling bundle configuration data. It is commonly used for setting up port allocations, setting URLs, and other variables. Use this service aide in providing a dynamic execution environment. |
| Declarative Services | A component model is used to simplify making components that publish or reference OSGi services. |
| Deployment Admin | This provides standardized access to the life cycle management of resources in an OSGi environment. This service helps to maintain the overall consistency of the runtime. |
| Device Access | This service coordinates adding and removing devices, and provisioning of their drivers. This helps to facilitate a hot deploy, or a plug and play model. |
| DMT Admin | A generic Device Management Tree API is provided to manage devices by mapping the generic tree to specific device functions. |
| Event Admin | This is a high-capacity event service for inter-bundle communication utilizing a publish and subscribe model. |

| OSGi Compendium Service | Purpose |
| --- | --- |
| Foreign Application Access | This service provides a mechanism to allow non-OSGi Java applications to interoperate with the OSGi environment. |
| HTTP | The HTTP service provides support for registering servlets and resources. This allows users to access, retrieve information from, and control the OSGi environment. |
| Initial Provisioning | A specification that defines how a management agent becomes part of and interacts with the OSGi environment. |
| IO Connector | This is a basic communication infrastructure based on the J2ME `javax.microedition.io` package. |
| Metatype | This allows services to specify datatypes they can use. Key/value pairs are used to represent data attributes. |
| Monitor Admin | It defines how a bundle may publish status variables, and how administrative bundles can discover and use their values. |
| Preferences | It provides bundles as a mechanism to persist data through starting and stopping of the bundle, or of the OSGi environment. This service is not intended for large quantities of data such as documents or images, but for preferences or setting values (properties). |
| User Admin | This service manages the persistent storage of user credentials, and their attributes, providing an authentication service for end users and/or devices that need to initiate actions in the OSGi environment. |
| UPnPTM | It defines how the OSGi environment can interoperate with **Universal Plug and Play (UPnPTM)** devices and control points. |
| Wire Admin | An administrative service that provides control over the dynamic wiring of producers to their consumers in an OSGi environment. |
| XML Parser | This service covers how classes in JAXP can be used in an OSGi environment. |

While the preceding table is helpful in quickly understanding the OSGi compendium, we feel that we should look a little closer at the Blueprint Container and Configuration Admin.

## Blueprint Container

OSGi Service Platform Release 4 Version 4.2 specifications introduced the Blueprint Container specification.

This specification describes how declarative programming and dependency injection is done in an OSGi container. There are two separate implementations of the Blueprint specification, one from the Apache Foundation—Apache Aries Blueprint—as well as one from the Eclipse Foundation—Eclipse Gemini. The examples in this book and the demonstration code were tested using the Apache Aries version.

Blueprint is built around an OSGi extender pattern. Once a bundle has resolved its dependencies, it is up to the Blueprint extender to do the following:

✦ Parse the Blueprint XML files

✦ Instantiate recipes

✦ Wire the components together

✦ Manage services' registrations

✦ Look up service references

A Blueprint file's basic building blocks are the beans, shown as follows:

```xml
<?xml version="1.0" encoding="UTF-8"?>
<blueprint xmlns="http://www.osgi.org/xmlns/blueprint/v1.0.0">
    <bean id="accountOne" class="org.apache.aries.simple.Account" />
</blueprint>
```

Beans can also have properties; these properties can be references or values, as shown in the following screenshot:

```xml
<bean id="accountOne" class="org.apache.aries.simple.Account">
    <property name="currency" ref="currency" />
</bean>

<bean id="currency" class="org.apache.aries.simple.Currency" />
```

A Blueprint Container also provides a model for interaction with the OSGi service registry allowing you to define beans that can then be exported.

```xml
<service id="serviceOne" ref="account"
 interface="org.apache.aries.simple.Account" />

<bean id="account" class="org.apache.aries.simple.AccountImpl" />
```

As seen from earlier examples, services are exported and found via their interface class.

Once we have a service that we want to consume, we can do so from another bundle by referencing it across the service registry with a reference tag, as follows:

```
<bean id="accountClient" class="...">
    <property name="account" ref="accountRef" />
</bean>

<reference id="accountRef" interface="org.apache.aries.simple.Account"
```

These are the basic building blocks in Blueprint; the specification also provides for namespace handlers so that developers can extend the container with a specific behavior for named beans. This is used quite extensively in projects such as Apache Camel, Apache CXF, and of course Apache Aries.

Utilizing the namespace handler techniques, the container is enriched with web service wiring, context resolution, configuration admin integration, and property injection.

## Configuration Admin

One of the most powerful of all services in the OSGi environment is the Configuration Admin service. It is a "merge" between the simple paradigm of reading configuration data at startup time combined with the fact that the said data can and will change during an application's life cycle. In a fully dynamic environment, your configuration can change at any time and you're expected to react to these changes; the Configuration Admin API classes allow you to do exactly this; your bundles will be notified of new, updated, and removed configuration data.

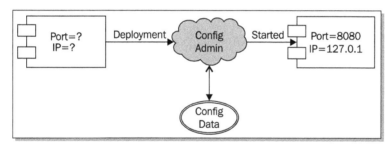

This also allows for some very useful patterns you can build on top of `org.osgi.service.cm.Managed ServiceFactories`. Apache Felix provides configuration interfaces via `fileinstall` as well as the `webconsole`.

# 5 – OSGI and modular patterns

In this section we'll discuss several OSGI and modular programming patterns that we believe you should follow, which will help in producing successful projects.

## Whiteboard pattern

A whiteboard pattern is a very well documented pattern that has a detailed description on the OSGi forum, http://www.osgi.org/wiki/uploads/Links/whiteboard.pdf. It is somewhat similar to an extender pattern but relies on the OSGi service registry instead of raw bundles.

### Idea

Java has, since 1.0, had an event platform. These events unfortunately could lead to fairly cumbersome development cycles with more than 130 events and adapters available already in Java 1.3. The whiteboard pattern provides events in a simple manner without forcing a listener pattern to be implemented. This is done relying on the OSGi service registry for informational messages and further processing.

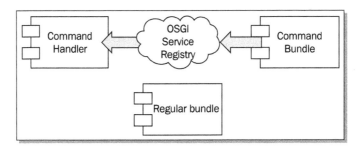

### Implementation

A whiteboard pattern in its simplest form is implemented via BundleActivator and the registration of a ServiceTracker object at http://www.osgi.org/javadoc/r4v42/org/osgi/util/tracker/ServiceTracker.html.

ServiceTracker gives us an implementation that correctly handles all the details of listening to ServiceEvents and getting and ungetting services. It is also a thread-safe class so it will aid bundle developers in what otherwise would be a fairly cumbersome process involving quite a bit of manual checking of services and registrations.

The whiteboard service tracker bundle subscribes to service registration information, as shown in the following screenshot:

```
public EventAdminListener(BundleContext context) {
    tracker = new ServiceTracker(context, HttpServlet.class.getName(), null);
    tracker.open();
}
```

Here we are registering `ServiceTracker` on a bundle context, we give it an `HttpServlet` interface to match against and by providing a null as the last argument we are saying that we want to be notified of every single event.

With our listener installed, we are now ready to start looking for these services being added, removed, suspended, and so on. If we say that a servlet example would be deployed in blueprint for the sake of argument, that deployment would look something like the following screenshot:

```
<blueprint xmlns="http://www.osgi.org/xmlns/blueprint/v1.0.0">
    <service interface="javax.servlet.http.HttpServlet">
        <service-properties>
            <entry key="alias" value="/myservlet"/>
        </service-properties>
        <bean id="myServlet" class="com.example.MyServlet"/>
    </service>
</blueprint>
```

It would now be up to our `ServiceTracker` bundle to grab this service, and publish this in a servlet container under the path `/myservlet`.

As you can see, this is a very graceful, not to mention useful, "Factory" instantiation pattern that will allow for full dynamism, thanks to the nature of OSGi bundles and the service registry.

### Common uses

Whiteboard patterns are used quite frequently in OSGi. Some examples would be generic commands, such as the original PAX web extender for servlet enhancement of an OSGi container. Refer to `http://karaf.apache.org/manual/2.2.6/users-guide/http.html`.

# Extender pattern

The OSGi extender pattern is one of the most used and implemented strategies for framework enhancement. It is a pattern that models itself towards extensive enhancement of deployments and is used to provide EE behavior in the core of many of today's most advanced Java containers. An extender pattern allows the enhancing of bundles with a custom life cycle that will react as bundles come and go. Prominent implementations of the extender pattern are Apache Aries Blueprint and Spring Dynamic Modules; they both rely on this pattern to control their application participants.

## Idea

The basic idea around the extender pattern is for the developer of the "extender" to take advantage of the event information and life cycle inherently available to a bundle. We know when a bundle is resolved, we know when it is started, and we know when it is starting. This all leads us to using the OSGi container and runtime; we utilize all of the information we get from the environment to allow us to control and influence the life cycle of other bundles. These bundles in turn provide the extender with custom information, such as OSGi headers or XML files placed in a specific location.

## Implementation

The OSGi life cycle allows a bundle, very much like the activator, to participate and listen to events regarding the installation, update, and removal of other bundles. This life cycle is dynamic in nature. If we were to just gather the event information, we'd do so utilizing a normal `org.osgi.framework.BundleListener` interface. Refer to http://www.osgi.org/javadoc/r4v43/core/org/osgi/framework/BundleListener.html.

The regular `BundleListener` is an asynchronous ordered implementation that cannot be called concurrently; it is up to the framework to call our `BundleListener` interface and dispatch information to us. As seen from this description, the `BundleListener` interface lends itself to logging and informational purposes but there is also `org.osgi.framework.SynchronousBundleListener`. Refer to http://www.osgi.org/javadoc/r4v43/core/org/osgi/framework/SynchronousBundleListener.html.

This listener actually allows us to take an action on these events, as seen in `JavaDocs` for this class. Unlike normal `BundleListener` objects, `SynchronousBundleListeners` are synchronously called during bundle life cycle processing.

The bundle life cycle processing will not proceed until all `SynchronousBundleListeners` have completed. `SynchronousBundleListener` objects will be called prior to `BundleListener` objects. The following diagram shows the extender pattern:

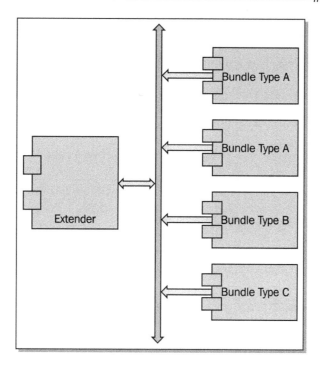

Armed with this class, we suddenly have a fairly powerful mechanism for building completely new flows for our bundles. If we go back to the Apache Aries Blueprint mentioned earlier, in essence it is really a listener, and when our bundle goes active, it will look for files in `OSGI-INF/blueprint` ending in `.xml`.

The synchronous invocation gives us the ability to do things before the actual event has passed. So we can perform initialization, register services, evaluate files, check for resources, and manipulate bundle information so that we can fully take control of the execution environment.

Depicted on the left, the extender bundle that is controlling the flow of information is going to utilize `org.osgi.framework.BundleEvent` as it receives and looks for bundles containing Type A information. Once it finds a matching bundle, the extender has control of the bundle providing the event, so it can instantiate classes, set up application contexts, and register further metadata and information before handing back control of the event to the framework.

## Common uses

The extender pattern is used to implement Apache Aries Blueprint, Spring Dynamic Modules as well as Apache Felix Declarative services. It is typically used to extend functionality into an OSGi container. A slight word of caution should be raised as it can become something of a slight anti-pattern, especially if the extenders start manipulating the normal class-loading mechanisms or startup sequencing.

# People and places you should get to know

If you need help with OSGi, here are some people and places that will prove invaluable.

## Official sites

The following is a list of important sites, which will prove useful:

+ **Home page**: `http://www.osgi.org` is the official home page of the OSGi Alliance.

+ **Manual and documentation**: `http://www.osgi.org/Specifications/HomePage`. The OSGI specifications represent the most in-depth explanation of OSGi available to developers.

+ **Wiki**: `http://wiki.osgi.org/wiki/Main_Page`. The OSGi Alliance maintains a community wiki.

+ **Blog**: `http://blog.osgi.org/` is the OSGi Alliance blog stream.

+ **Source code**: The OSGi Alliance maintains the specification for an OSGI environment, while other projects provide implementations. Two popular implementations are Apache Felix and Eclipse Equinox. The Apache Felix source code can be found at `http://svn.apache.org/repos/asf/felix/trunk`, while the Eclipse Equinox source can be found at `http://dev.eclipse.org/viewcvs/viewvc.cgi`.

## Articles and tutorials

The following is a list of important tutorial sites, which will prove useful:

+ **Apache Felix tutorial series**:
  `http://felix.apache.org/site/apache-felix-osgi-tutorial.html`

+ **Peter Krien's series on BND Tool**:
  `http://www.aqute.biz/Bnd/Bnd`

+ **OSGi with Eclipse Equinox Tutorial**:
  `http://www.vogella.com/articles/OSGi/article.html`

+ **Listeners considered harmful**: The "whiteboard" pattern:
  `http://www.osgi.org/wiki/uploads/Links/whiteboard.pdf`

+ **A beginners tutorial series**:
  `http://www.javaworld.com/javaworld/jw-03-2008/jw-03-osgi1.html`

## Community

The following is a list of important community sites, which will prove useful:

+ **Official mailing list sign up**: `https://mail.osgi.org/mailman/listinfo/interest`
+ **Official forums**: `http://www.osgi.org/Forums/HomePage`
+ **User FAQ**: `http://www.osgi.org/About/FAQ`

## Blogs

The following is a list of important blogs, which will prove useful:

+ The blog of Peter Kriens, former technical director of OSGI:
  `http://softwaresimplexity.blogspot.com`
+ Felix Meschberger is the current Apache Felix PMC Chairperson:
  `http://blog.meschberger.ch`
+ Neil Bartlet is among the most influential people in the OSGi community.
  His blog can be found here: `http://njbartlett.name`

## Twitter

Some useful Twitter handles are as follows:

+ Follow OSGi Alliance: `http://twitter.com/#!/osgialliance`
+ Follow Peter Kriens: `http://twitter.com/#!/pkriens`
+ Follow Neil Bartlett: `https://twitter.com/#!/njbartlett`
+ For more Open Source information, follow Packt at
  `http://twitter.com/#!/packtopensource`

## About Packt Publishing

Packt, pronounced 'packed', published its first book "*Mastering phpMyAdmin for Effective MySQL Management*" in April 2004 and subsequently continued to specialize in publishing highly focused books on specific technologies and solutions.

Our books and publications share the experiences of your fellow IT professionals in adapting and customizing today's systems, applications, and frameworks. Our solution based books give you the knowledge and power to customize the software and technologies you're using to get the job done. Packt books are more specific and less general than the IT books you have seen in the past. Our unique business model allows us to bring you more focused information, giving you more of what you need to know, and less of what you don't.

Packt is a modern, yet unique publishing company, which focuses on producing quality, cutting-edge books for communities of developers, administrators, and newbies alike. For more information, please visit our website: www.packtpub.com.

## Writing for Packt

We welcome all inquiries from people who are interested in authoring. Book proposals should be sent to author@packtpub.com. If your book idea is still at an early stage and you would like to discuss it first before writing a formal book proposal, contact us; one of our commissioning editors will get in touch with you.

We're not just looking for published authors; if you have strong technical skills but no writing experience, our experienced editors can help you develop a writing career, or simply get some additional reward for your expertise.

www.ingramcontent.com/pod-product-compliance
Lightning Source LLC
LaVergne TN
LVHW080105070326
832902LV00014B/2436